A Trip to the Ch

Near Bangor, and Other Par

Anonymous

Alpha Editions

This edition published in 2024

ISBN : 9789362092243

Design and Setting By
Alpha Editions
www.alphaedis.com
Email - info@alphaedis.com

As per information held with us this book is in Public Domain.
This book is a reproduction of an important historical work. Alpha Editions uses the best technology to reproduce historical work in the same manner it was first published to preserve its original nature. Any marks or number seen are left intentionally to preserve its true form.

Contents

A TRIP TO THE CHAIN-BRIDGE, &c. &c. ....- 1 -
APPENDIX, ...- 15 -
    PENMAEN-MAWR. ....- 15 -
    PUFFIN ISLAND, OR PRIESTHOLME. ....- 15 -
    PENRHYN CASTLE. ....- 15 -
    BEAUMARIS. ....- 15 -
    BANGOR. ....- 16 -
    THE CHAIN-BRIDGE. ....- 16 -
    CARNARVON. ....- 16 -
    DOL BADERN CASTLE. ....- 16 -
    SNOWDON. ....- 16 -
    CONWAY. ....- 17 -
    CAPEL CERIG. ....- 17 -
    BEDDGELERT. ....- 17 -
    THE GRAVE OF THE GREYHOUND. ....- 18 -

A TRIP TO THE CHAIN-BRIDGE, &c. &c.

I had never been in Wales beyond the border counties of Flint, Denbigh, and Montgomery, and was, of course, a stranger to the best scenery of the Principality. Business, however, required that I should visit some parts of the north-west, and as curiosity prompted me to see the new Chain-bridge over the straits of Menai, I determined upon commencing my trip from Liverpool by the Llewellyn steam-packet; and, accordingly, on Tuesday, the 26th July, about ten o'clock in the forenoon, I embarked on board that fine vessel, which was just on the point of weighing anchor. The river Mersey was a scene of general bustle, the liveliness of which was heightened by the brightness of the sun, and the beauty of a fleecy sky. A light breeze from the northward gave freshness to the air; every appearance was favourable to such an excursion as I had projected; and a goodly company, assembling on all parts of the vessel's deck, indicated that "*all the world and his wife*" were in a rambling humour this summer. Amongst other objects on the river an arrival from Dublin suddenly attracted universal attention. A steam-ship came close past us with such a cargo as I never before beheld, although in the summer season there may be many such. There were probably between seven and eight hundred persons, chiefly Irish harvest-labourers, standing on the deck of the vessel, as closely packed as the crowd at a town meeting; and so much did this upper weight preponderate in the balance against the cargo (if any) below, that the vessel continually heeled, or swayed, from one side to the other to such a degree, that her gangway ladder at one moment touched a boat alongside, and at another arose out of the boatman's reach. The crowd on board were alternately visible, as on an inclined plane, towards each shore, as if the vessel were proud of its miserable cargo, and was determined that the farmers both in Lancashire and Cheshire, should be apprized of the arrival of the poor reapers. It was an advertisement for them, free of duty. In a few minutes our engine commenced its herculean labours, and, amidst the exchange of kind wavings of the hand between us and our friends on shore, we began, not to sail, for we had no canvas extended, but, to use a sailor's phrase, to "*plough the deep.*"

The passengers on board were about a hundred and seventy in number, chiefly of the most respectable classes. Sir R. W. and a part of his family were under the awning on the quarterdeck, as was also a worthy alderman, T. C. and many others. Among those on the fore part of the deck was the veteran comedian R., the author of that amusing work "The Itinerant." A Dublin gentleman and myself became his companions till we reached Beaumaris, and we found, as I frequently have found, much pleasure in his agreeable society. About the middle of the deck was stationed a small but good band of musicians, who, from time to time, performed almost all the favourite airs of the present day; and among the passengers standing about the bowsprit was a small knot of friends, apparently choristers in some country church, who, in the intervals between the other musical performances, sang, in very good style, several chaunts, psalms, and anthems. Ranged under the fore gunwale of the vessel, and sitting on the deck, were several Welsh market-women; who, as there were no novel sights for them to gaze upon, seemed disposed to "while away the sunny day" in slumber, or in quiet conversation with each other; while the busier throng about them, many of whom had never before been on the *"salt sea ocean,"* were eagerly watching for objects worthy of notice and inquiry. The scenery on both sides of the river, the Rock Perch, the rocks and caverns called the Red Noses, the several lighthouses, the vessels approaching or departing, or gliding on the horizon, the Floating-light, the Welsh mountains, and the clear deep green colour of the sea, became successively the topics of observation, and the sources of pleasure; nor, amongst a select few, were Helbre Island and "King Robert" forgotten. The singers attended to their singing, the musicians to their music, and the cook to his cooking. Appetite was the principal ailment on board, although, gently be it spoken, some few of the passengers, smooth as the sea was, were seen creeping into corners, and "casting up their accounts." In general, the ready snack, and the bottle of porter, were in great requisition; while a considerable number of persons sat down in the cabin to a regular half-crown dinner, and a glass of good port. All this time we made great progress on the water, a couple of sails having been recently hoisted in aid of our steam-power; and we soon passed that grand object, the Great Ormshead, which must be terrific indeed to the crew of any vessel placed near its rugged and threatening front, in a strong north-west wind. Penmaen-mawr soon appeared on our left, bold and rugged as the Ormshead, but much loftier. Like an ornamental band passing along his front, a little above his base, we saw what was pointed out to us as the great mail-road between Conway and Bangor. Neither this road, nor the hill itself, appeared so elevated as I expected; but this I afterwards found was owing to our great distance from the shore, which, although several miles off, appeared very near; the sea being quite smooth, and there being no intermediate objects by which we could calculate distances. Puffin Island, with the east coast of Anglesea behind it, was now right a-head of us, and the opening of Beaumaris Bay a little to the left. We proceeded in that direction, passing large flights of puffins, and shortly entered that beautiful bay, with Penrhyn Castle on our left; Beaumaris, its Castle, and Lady Bulkeley's Park on the right; and the town of Bangor, and the straits of Menai immediately before us. Opposite Beaumaris, at a quarter before five o'clock, the packet stopped a few minutes, boats approached us, and I and several other persons landed, including Sir R. W., whose carriage was waiting to convey him, and the ladies with him, to his seat in the neighbourhood; and including also Mr. M., his two sisters, and two other young ladies, whom I shall have occasion frequently to mention again. The neat little town of Beaumaris, (the capital of Anglesea,) the Castle, which is a beautiful ruin, and the adjoining Park, are well worth the stranger's attention. Being anxious to proceed further that night, and having transacted some business in the town, and taken tea at the King's Arms, I was ready at seven o'clock to join a party, if I could meet with one, in hiring a boat for Bangor, three miles across the water, or to the Chain-bridge, two miles further, or to Carnarvon, seven miles beyond it. The boatmen spoke of a party going to Bangor, but not further, that night. I met the party coming to the beach. It was Mr. M. and the four ladies. They seemed pleased, and I am sure I was, to find that we were all going the same way, and they politely received me as one of their party. I pointed out to them a glimpse of the Chain-bridge in the distance, and proposed that, if the boatmen would take us, we should proceed through the straits all the way to Carnarvon that night, the wind and tide being completely favourable. This was instantly and gladly agreed to, as suiting, and, indeed, advancing their purposes as well as mine; fifteen silvery reasons satisfied the boatmen; and our merrily-disposed little party of six were seated in the boat, the sails set, and the oars at work, at a quarter-past seven o'clock.

It was a lovely evening. The ladies' parasols were, at first, in requisition; but, in a short time, the higher ground of the Anglesea coast afforded us a more general shade, and then the beauty of the scene around us was indescribable. On our left, Port Penrhyn, with its immense inn, and the city of Bangor in the hollow, were broadly lighted by the declining sun. The tints on the neighbouring mountains were finer than I ever beheld; and they were so rich, that a faithful picture of them would be considered too highly coloured. Every moment brought us nearer to the stupendous work I have before alluded to—the Chain-bridge, which I shall hereafter more particularly describe. Near its western extremity lay, at anchor, in calm repose, the steam-packet which had recently been so busily employed. We looked up to the suspended chain-work of the bridge, which, at first, had appeared light and elegant, but which, the nearer we approached, assumed a heavier and grander appearance; and we saw several persons moving to and fro upon it, whose apparently diminutive stature and dangerous situation surprised, and almost pained us. The boatmen here brailed up the sails, preparatory to our passing the *swellies*, as they called them, which are a series of circling eddies, caused by abrupt rocks under the water, just beyond the new bridge, and about the centre of the straits. We passed under the lofty chains of the bridge, amazed with their height and length, and with the vast strength of the granite pillars and arches on each shore, from which the chains are suspended. We soon entered the swellies, where circles, caused by the under-rocks, whirled on every side, the surface of the water being broken in places by other rocks which rose above its level. Here the stream, however, was still in our favour, and was so exceedingly rapid that we felt as if moved along by an unseen power. In a short time we came into almost still water, but the current gradually increased again: we had come, so far, with the stream from the sea at Beaumaris; the tide was now running from the centre of the straits to the sea at Carnarvon, the breeze was as before, and our canvas was again spread, so that we were not detained by wind or wave a single moment. The column, erected in honour of the Marquis of Anglesea, here formed a prominent object on a hill towards the west; and not far from us the splendid seat of the Marquis was the grace and ornament of the lower and richly-wooded ground. The appearance of the glassy water was now particularly fine. The red clouds above us flung down the rays which they caught from the setting sun, and their reflection represented rocks of bright coral beneath us, while the rising moon cast her pale light into the wave, forming the semblance of a pyramidal rock of polished silver. A number of young cranes stood on the shore, at respectful distances from each other, earnestly gazing at us as we glided smoothly by. Observations on all we witnessed, together with anecdote and poetry, prevailed amongst us throughout the scene; and never, certainly, were better timed the vocal efforts of some of the party, in duets, such as "*Flow on, thou shining river,*" "*The Canadian Boat Song,*" and "*O come to me when day-light sets.*" Foreign scenery was described; poets and travellers were quoted; and our stores of conversation were increased by the circumstance that the brother of one of the ladies present had been with the lamented Belzoni, in the latter days, and at the death, of that enterprising traveller. We appeared to be upon a lake in fairy land; and after two hours of the most delightful sailing I ever enjoyed, we stepped upon shore under the picturesque walls of Carnarvon. At Parry's handsome and well situated hotel we were most comfortably accommodated; our sitting-room overlooked the "moonlight sea," and commanded a view of Anglesea. The ladies, after partaking with us of a slight refreshment, retired to rest, while Mr. M. and myself proceeded to view the celebrated ruins of Carnarvon Castle, which were then beautifully illuminated by the sweet heavenly lamp of night. These ruins have been so often described, that it is unnecessary for me to say more of them than that they very far exceed in extent and majesty of appearance any idea I had formed of them from paintings or description. They were truly interesting, and almost awful, to contemplate. Returning to our inn, we passed through the north gate, near which some vessels are being built and repaired; and here both of us were struck with a most extraordinary appearance in the sky. The last red tinges were fading from the western clouds; but an arch, apparently of sun-light, seemed to hang over the scene of the recent departure of day. The arch was about fifty degrees broad, and twenty in height, from the horizon. It was very bright, and strongly defined; its ends appeared to rest upon two bright, but ill defined and short, pillars, while the centre was supported by a magnificent column of vivid light. Between the pillars, all was total darkness for several moments, but in a short time streaks of light in parallel lines to the pillars, began to descend from the arch, from south to north; the whole then vanished gradually but rapidly, and the still and silvery moonlight now extended, unopposed, to where a scene had just occurred more strange, varied, beautiful, and flitting, than even the powers of magic could adequately describe. It was now near eleven o'clock, and we adjourned to our respective apartments, wondering at how much we had done, and how much we had seen to admire, in the twelve short hours which had elapsed since we left the Mersey.

Next morning the weather was still extremely fine, and at an early hour we accompanied the ladies in visiting the Castle, the interior of which, the gloomy passages, the massy towers, and the fine view from the top, afforded us much scope for speculative observation, and for pretty active exertion. Of course, the little guide did not omit to point out the room in which Edward II. was born, nor which were the courtly and which the military departments of the place.

After our party had enjoyed a substantial breakfast at the hotel, I proceeded into the town for an hour or two to transact some business, the only remarkable feature of which was my receiving payment of a debt of above nine years' standing, from a person I never knew. During this time a handsome open sociable and a pair of horses were got ready, for a few hours' excursion. The hotels at Carnarvon are well supplied with convenient cars and sociables, the latter being adapted to the comfortable accommodation of six persons. By the bye, I may here mention, that six appears to be the best number for a party making a tour such as that I am describing; for whether in boats, or in vehicles on shore, the sixth part of the cost of conveyance is extremely reasonable; while, at the same time, six persons are as comfortably accommodated as three or four. About eleven o'clock we set out for the lakes of Lan-berris, proceeding a little way by the Beddgellert road, making a call at Penrhos, the residence of R. H. W. Esq. and then crossing the country towards the lakes. The approach to the lower or principal lake is rugged and hilly, and we left our carriage at the summit of a piece of high ground just before we descended into the vale, a boatman having there met us, offering his services. The view from a stile on our right hand was here truly delightful, and came upon us quite by surprise. The lake which lay shining before us, a very picturesque bridge crossing it near its lower extremity, and the almost Alpine appearance of the surrounding mountains, with Snowdon's venerable summit in the distance, formed a picture at once interesting and sublime. We proceeded to the foot of the lake, and seated ourselves in a small boat, in which the boatman and his wife immediately began to use the oars very dexterously. "Row, *brothers*, row," would here have been out of place; but "*the Vale of Ovoca*" was vividly present to our minds, and our ears enjoyed a vocal remembrancer of it. The water in the lake seemed unusually low, owing to the long continued drought; for, until we reached the bridge I have before mentioned, our boat frequently touched the clear pebbly bottom, or rustled through the long and beautiful verdure which grew beneath the surface of the water, and which, by a constant inclination towards the termination of the lake, indicated the direction of the placid stream. At one time the boatman stepped into the water, and dragged the boat easily along. We soon passed the bridge, under the low arches of which several cows were enjoying the luxuries of a cool shade and a foot bath. From this portal we entered at once upon the deep and broad expanse of the lake, and our boatman made himself very communicative with respect to any remarkable spot, or incident, within his knowledge. Snowdon, and the other mountains around, cast their varied shadows upon the water; the sun shone in meridian splendour; and we glided merrily along, occasionally refreshing ourselves with a handful of water from the sweet and crystal element on which we floated. All around was loveliness and happiness; and it was pleasing, though not at all surprising, to see, that when the ladies averted their eyes from other attractions, and looked into the brilliant abyss below, four handsome blooming faces gazed smilingly up at them. Dol Badern Castle, or rather tower, now became a prominent object, crowning the head of the lake; and we landed to the right of it, upon the banks of a meadow, through which we passed to the only inn in the neighbourhood, where we enjoyed some refreshment, and where our boatman and his "*help meet*" who had rowed us about three miles, and were to row us back again, for six shillings, were not forgotten.

From the inn we walked, shaded from the hot sun by umbrellas and parasols, to the junction of the upper and lower lakes, near the foot of Dol Barden Tower. A good looking, but meanly-dressed boy, who seemed to guess at our object, here placed himself just before us, and slowly walked up to the tower, by the most direct road. We followed him, and ascended to the castle terrace, which commanded a fine view of the lower, and a portion of the upper lake; but we were excluded, by a part of the building, from a full view of the entire vale. In a few moments our little guide, whom we had scarcely missed, peeped out upon us from an upper window of the ruined tower. He could not tell us how he got there, because he could not utter a word of English; but we were much surprised, when, after another momentary disappearance, we saw him looking down upon us from the very top of the tower. Two of our enterprising ladies determined upon following him, if possible; and we discovered, that, by climbing through a window-place, above the steps of the terrace, access could be obtained to what was once, no doubt, a convenient spiral staircase. They climbed the place, followed by

Mr. M. and myself, who were astonished at their intrepidity in ascending the building, which consisted of a pretty large circular tower, with small shattered steps, leading spirally up the interior of the walls to the top, without any rail or any central support whatever, and where the least slip must have cost life or limb. Up, however, they and we proceeded; and, when we reached the top, and sat down upon the main wall of the ruins, the panorama was, indeed, complete: the entire valley, the two lakes, and the surrounding mountains and quarries, were all in broad display around us, while the thunder-like reports of explosions in the distant slate-rocks, and the echoes they occasioned from the hills, heightened the interest of the gratifying scene. The ladies (and perhaps the gentlemen, too) felt a momentary fear, respecting the descent they had to make; but our little guide, who ran about the tops of the steep walls like a cat, seemed to show us so good an example of coolness of mind, that, after advising each other to steadiness and carefulness, we descended in safety, and rewarded the little silent boy for his unsought voluntary guidance. We then returned to our inn, and, in a short time, proceeded to our boat, meeting, in our way, the worthy Alderman T. C. whom I have before mentioned, and also W. S. Esq. the T. C. of a certain "*good old town*," with his family. We had a short conversation with them upon some local matters, amongst which, the merits and claims of a certain Mechanics' Institute were not omitted. We then set out on our return. During our stay at the inn, we had some idea of ascending Snowdon; but we found, on calculation, that it would be too great a task for that day, and that, to stay during the night at the inn, in order to ascend the mountain at the best time, namely, at sun-rise, would disarrange our plans. All the party, however, except myself, whom business prevented, agreed to return to the inn on the following night, and make the ascent at dawn the succeeding morning. I must here remark that Snowdon does not appear so lofty from the lake as a stranger would expect: but this is owing, no doubt, to the nearness and bulk of the surrounding hills, and the uncertainty, to the eye, of the actual distance of that lord of the mountains. On the road to Carnarvon, we were particularly struck with the forwardness of the grain crops, which appeared a fortnight in advance, compared with those of Lancashire and Cheshire. We arrived at the hotel in the evening, and sat down, at seven o'clock, to an excellent dinner, including some choice fish, and by far the tenderest and best mutton we ever tasted. As we were now in "*foreign parts abroad*", we managed, amongst us, a bottle of good port, and drank to the healths of "*all friends in England.*" In the evening we ordered fresh horses to our sociable, and were quickly conveyed, by moonlight, over a fine road, and through a beautiful country, to Bangor, where, at the Liverpool Arms, we met with pleasant looks, good entertainment, and comfortable repose.

On the following morning the weather was as beautiful as ever, and as my time was more limited than that of my companions, I resolved to proceed to the Chain-bridge and back before breakfast. Mr. M. was kind enough to join me, and, in a few minutes, there was ready for us a one horse car, similar to those so much used in Dublin, and called outside cars. It was capable of accommodating six persons, besides the driver, and was altogether a comfortable vehicle. We soon reached the summit of the elevated ground between the city and the bridge, and then, looking to the northward, on our right, we enjoyed a magnificent view of the whole bay of Beaumaris, and of all the prominent objects by which its beautiful neighbourhood is distinguished. Descending from this point, past the ferry-house, we immediately arrived at the shore, and then turning to the left, we ascended a slope till we reached the level of the road-way of the new bridge, one hundred feet above high-water mark. Here we stood near one of the great suspending piers, whose foundation is more than one hundred feet below, and whose summit is fifty-two feet above, the level of the road. Two arched gate-ways are formed through this gigantic structure, leading to the two intended carriage-ways across the straits. Over the apex of this pier, the four massy chains hang in firm but graceful festoon. We traced them nearly to their fastenings in the rocks, and were astonished at the amazing strength and security of the whole work. Between the fastenings and the pier we noticed the erection of what seemed designed for the toll-house; a handsome building, rising up to, and amongst the chains, as if the bridge were to derive its *support* (and perhaps it will) from the *toll* house. We walked up the chains to the top of this building, and thence to the apex of the pier, where our elevation, one hundred and fifty-two feet above the water, appeared somewhat terrific.

I may here remark that the four chains are thus formed of solid bars of wrought iron. Each bar is about ten feet long, about three inches broad, and one inch thick. Five of these bars placed upon their edges, with fastenings at the ends, which keep them more than an inch asunder, form a straight link, a series of which links, to the length of 1714 feet, constitutes a single chain. Four such chains, placed one above the other, the joints of one chain falling on the centre of the links of the next, form *one great chain*, containing, of course, twenty solid bars, the pressure upon each of which will be equalized by connecting stanchions.

Each carriage-way, twelve feet wide, will be supported by two of these great chains; and there will be a foot-path along the centre. I have here described such links as are placed between the two piers and crossing the straits; those from the piers to the fastenings are rather shorter and thicker. The two centre chains, below which the foot-path will be formed, between the carriage-ways, are, of course, near to each other; perhaps not three feet asunder. Between these two chains lay our path over the straits; a temporary path, formed of planks, two in a breadth, suspended from the lower links, the upper ones serving as a sort of hand-rail.

From the apex on which we sat, the chains appeared to descend very steeply towards their fastenings on the land side, and towards the centre over the straits. Although the planks were not properly fastened, we proceeded fearlessly along the vast curvature, 590 feet in length, to the pier on the Anglesea side. Over the centre of the straits we sat down on a small stage, which had been placed there for the band of musicians on the day when the last chain was suspended. From this place, looking downwards, we observed that the colour of the water appeared to be a muddy pea-green. On the apex of the Anglesea pier we had some conversation with one of the superintendents of the work, who obligingly showed us the rollers under the saddle of the chains, and the space in which they would move in case the contraction or expansion of the chains by cold or heat should ever become unequal on the two sides of the pier. Admiration of the stupendous and almost superhuman work, and of Mr. Telford's consummate skill, breathed in every observation we could make; and I thought that when death should deprive the country of the further services of that able engineer, his epitaph, simple as that upon Sir Christopher Wren, will be abundantly sufficient, if it state, that "*his monument is suspended over the Straits of Menai.*" The superintendent, while we remained on the "airy height," gave us much information relative to the proceedings of the workmen in their various arduous duties; and the only painful intelligence he communicated was, that four men had lost their lives, at different times, by falling from the elevated parts of the works. No accident, however, had happened to any of the numerous ladies and gentlemen who had recently passed over the chains. From the spot on which we stood we observed innumerable workmen completing the road to the bridge, and preparing the iron net-work which is to form the sides of the bridge, as soon as the carriage-ways are placed along the perpendicular suspenders from the chains.

After thanking our obliging informant, we descended the chains on the Anglesea side, and proceeded to the water's edge, to look at the archways formed under the road between the main pier and the land. These, which look so small in the printed views of the bridge, we found to be as broad and as lofty as the aisles of Cathedrals; being sixty-five feet in height, to the spring of the arches, and the span of each arch being fifty-two feet. We then walked towards the ferry, and the moment we reached it a boat was ready to cross the water. We embarked, hailed our distant charioteer by a shout, he answered us by waving his hat, and then driving down to meet us, and in a few minutes we were again seated in our car, jaunting towards Bangor, and anticipating the pleasure which awaited us in again meeting our fair friends, and in the enjoyment of a good breakfast.

We soon alighted at our inn, and over breakfast we recounted to the ladies all the particulars of our morning excursion. Some of them immediately expressed their determination to cross the chains on their intended visit to the bridge, that evening or the next day; indeed, they were adventurous enough for any thing. We found they had not been idle during our absence; and they afforded us an ample account of their walks about the Cathedral, and the environs of the city. After our repast, and after I had made two or three calls on business in the town, the car was again brought to the door, pursuant to our orders, with an extra horse, *à la tandem*, mounted by a youthful postillion, under the command of our driver. About ten o'clock we all took our seats in the commodious vehicle, and we're speedily whisked along, upon the road to Conway, under the brilliance and heat of a sun which rendered the ladies' parasols almost invaluable. As we proceeded we admired very much the gates of Penryn Park, which are quite out of the common style; and, as we approached Penmaen-mawr, the truly grand view of Beaumaris Bay on our left, with Puffin Island in the distance, the mountainous elevations on our right, and the fresh sea-breeze gently blowing on our faces, and all around us were quite delightful. The cool clear waves were rippling along the shore beneath us, and curling over the pebbly margin, as if to refresh us by their playful agitation. We met Pomona in the shape of a poor "Welse umman," carrying a small basket filled with tempting grapes; we relieved her of part of her burden, much to her satisfaction; and, as we journeyed along, we discussed the merits of the grapes with much more taste than the fox in the fable did.

Presently we began to ascend the elevated part of the road, which, like one of Jupiter's belts, girds the bulk of Penmaen-mawr. We found it much higher from the sea than it appeared to be when we were on board the Llewellyn; the huge mountain close on our right, and the precipice from the road side to the water on our left, were steep almost as walls. While we stopped to enjoy the view, we threw several stones down towards the water, and were surprised on observing the length of time which elapsed before they disappeared in the waves. A party of Irish harvesters, who, we supposed, had landed at Holyhead, and were in search of employment, were here strolling along; they had a stock of bread with them, and the small streams which they passed afforded them water; but they begged of us, very earnestly and very persuasively, "a few coppers, with which to buy a morsel of *backy*." Descending towards the eastern foot of the mountain, and again rising up a very steep road, we began to feel the heat of the day to be rather oppressive: but we soon stopped at a small public-house, where we refreshed our horses with water, our drivers with beer, and ourselves with some excellent buttermilk of the real cut-throat kind. We then walked up the hill, having a deep romantic glen on the left, with a glimpse of Beaumaris Bay behind us, on our right some bold and rugged crags, and near the top, a mass of specimens, large and small, amongst which a mineralogist might spend many pleasant hours.

We resumed our seats in the car, and found a pretty level road for some distance. We saw before us the vale in which the river Conway meets the sea; and at length, between us and the water, we discerned what we all agreed was the very *beau ideal* of an ancient city and castle. It was Conway, which lay right before us and below us; our elevation affording us a delightful bird's-eye view of the whole place; and certainly its walls and turrets (completely inclosing all the houses) and the Castle with its numerous and beautifully formed towers, were the best realization we had ever beheld of the ideas formed by our reading of cities and castles, in the stories of antiquity. Conway is quite perfect in this respect, and we entered its gates with feelings of uncommon interest. The city lies entirely on the slope of the hill, and the Castle, which is at the lower and eastern side of it, almost touches the water. The whole is admirably situated, and every view around it is worthy of the painter's pencil. It was about half-past twelve when we arrived at the Castle Inn, where we put up. We thence proceeded immediately to view the Castle, the ruins of which are extremely extensive and grand. Near the entrance we were annoyed by a swarm of children, who rushed out of the neighbouring cottages, begging for "a ha'penny, pleace eu ma'am; a ha'penny, pleace eu sair;" words which they are taught to utter in a whining tone, and which they continue repeating as long as they dare follow a party of strangers, in defiance of any remonstrance on their parts. This is a very common nuisance in some parts of Wales, and it is a matter of regret that the cottagers do not foresee what a deep and lasting mischief they are doing to their children, by initiating them in such degrading practices. We were shown into the Castle, among the ruins of which we enjoyed a cool lounge for a considerable time, the ladies always taking the lead in searching after the picturesque and gloomy, among broken towers and staircases. The scene around us was that in which Monk Lewis has placed his drama of the Castle Spectre: and, certainly, a finer theatre for the adventures of Angela, Father Philip, Reginald, and the Ghost itself, could not have been chosen than Conway Castle must have been in the days of its glory, and in the times of chivalry, of romance, and of dark deeds. From the terrace, near the water, we had our first view of the piers, and other works in progress, for the small, but handsomely-designed Chain-bridge over the dangerous ferry of Conway; an improvement in which the public are deeply interested, and by which they will be materially benefited.

Soon after our return to the inn, the time arrived when my cheerful companions and I were to part; they on their return to Bangor (to meet the lady's brother whom I mentioned as having been with Belzoni) whence they would proceed on their expedition to the Chain-bridge and to the top of

Snowdon; and I on my way to Llanrwst and Llangollen. Our regret that we could not longer accompany each other seemed proportionate to the pleasure we had enjoyed since we met; and that, certainly, was glowing and unmixed, and will, doubtless, be memorable to us all. They took their seats in the car, and after many a hearty "good bye," they were soon out of sight. I then walked down to the water's edge, and crossed the ferry on business. On my return to Conway I was struck with the excellent design and situation of the Chain-bridge. The approach to it from the Denbighshire side is along a new-made terrace or breakwater, advancing across the greater part of the river's breadth, and, of course, confining the rapid stream to very narrow limits on the Carnarvonshire side. From this terrace the Chain-bridge will appear to be the grand entrance, under triumphal arches, to the Castle itself; and although, on coming close to that venerable structure, there is a sudden turn from it, leading directly to the town, I fancy a party of travellers would not regret, that, instead of being deposited within the naked and roofless walls of the Castle, they were handed into a small but comfortable parlour at the Castle Inn.

About five o'clock in the afternoon I hired a small car to convey me to Llanrwst, about twelve miles up the vale; and having lost my living companions, I amused myself with that pathetic but strange compound of religion and romance, the "Lights and Shadows of Scottish Life," from which I turned, ever and anon, to gaze upon the charming landscape through which I was passing, and at the lovely "lights and shadows" which the declining sun and the tinted mountains were casting upon it. So forward was the harvest in this fertile and extensive vale, that numbers of reapers were busy in the corn-fields; and on my arrival at Llanrwst I was informed that already (July 28) a loaf of new wheat had been baked there. In transacting some business at Llanrwst that evening I found that the absence of one individual would leave me a vacant hour from eight to nine o'clock; and, as I was desirous of taking that opportunity of refreshing myself by bathing in the Conway, a tradesman accompanied me and pointed out a deep and retired corner of the river, in which I laved myself in the warm and clear stream with great pleasure. My conductor, I found, had seen the world, and his range of conversation was not confined either to these realms or to India. Inquiring in the town respecting the prevailing religious sects there, I was told by an inhabitant that they were chiefly Churchmen, Methodists, and "Wess lions." From this classification I learned that the new connexion assume the name of Methodists almost exclusively, while the "Wess lions" are content with the title they derive from the name of the indefatigable and pious John Wesley.

The evening was extremely fine, and soon after nine o'clock I was ready to pursue my journey. As I had sent my luggage by coach direct from Bangor to Llangollen, I had no incumbrance; and I decided upon walking about four miles, to Bettws y Coed, a small place on the great Welsh road. On leaving Llanrwst, and crossing the bridge towards Gwydyr House and wood, I was much pleased with the beauty of the scenery up the river; scenery which forcibly reminded me of the exquisite Diorama of Holyrood Chapel. The unclouded moon was shining above the summits of the hills towards the south-east, and brightly illumined the left bank of the river, and all the neighbouring objects in that direction; while the thick and lofty wood on the right cast a broad dark shade over the lower ground, and over part of the bed of the river, which was dry, in consequence of the long-continued fair weather. In the midst of this dark shade, and on the dry pebbles of the river, two or three boys had kindled a small but brilliant fire; the reflection of which from their hands and faces, as they knelt around it, was highly picturesque. Passing through a part of the wood on the right, I soon reached the high road, and continued my solitary walk over ground I had never before trodden, till I arrived at Bettws y Coed, where I was accommodated with humble but cleanly lodgings, at an inn on the road side.

On the following morning, charming landscapes and a clear sky rendered every thing around me delightful; and at an early hour I set out towards Llangollen, upon one of the Holyhead and Shrewsbury coaches, with every disposition to enjoy the interesting scenery through which we had to pass, upon one of the finest roads, perhaps the very finest, in the world. Nor was I disappointed. The iron bridge, the hills on one hand, the deep ravines on the other, and the variety which every turn in the road afforded to the view, made the journey short and pleasant. At a place where we stopped a few moments, a poor "Welse umman" solicited our favours, asking very assiduously of each passenger, (and at the same time exhibiting the various products of her industry)—"D'you want a Welse wig?—d'you want a wool stockings?—d'you want a wool gloves?—d'you want a Welse wig?"—and so on, alternately; but the weather was not *harvest* weather to *her*, and she obtained no orders. Soon after we passed Kernioge, and while we were travelling at full speed, I was surprised by a poor woman getting up behind the coach, obtaining a footing among the passengers, and handing her hat round, not only to those near her, but to those in front, to whom she reached across the roof; nor did I perceive, until I was informed of the fact, that she was perfectly blind! She descended from the coach with the utmost ease; although such was our rapidity, that, in a few moments, she was left far behind us. Passing through Corwen, I reached Llangollen about one o'clock. The beauties of this place, or rather of the vale in which it is situated, are well known. The bridge, standing upon foundations furnished by nature itself, is always an object of admiration; and if the town and church were light coloured, so as to present a distinct contrast to the surrounding foliage, the whole would have a most charming appearance. So exhausted was the river

Dee at this season, that I crossed the timber of a small wear, and the bed of the river, without wetting even the soles of my shoes. From Llangollen, homewards, my journey was merely on business; but I thought, that, up to this period, a narrative of the incidents which had occurred during a trip of only three days and three hours' duration, might not be uninteresting to some of my friends.

APPENDIX,

Containing some particulars of Objects and Places mentioned in "The Trip."

Chiefly extracted from "The Cambrian Traveller's Guide," a large and useful volume, published by Mr. George Nicholson, of Stourport.

PENMAEN-MAWR.

This mountain is the terminating point of the long Carnarvonshire chain. It is 1550 feet high, from the level of the sea. As late as the year 1772 there was only a narrow and dangerous path along the shelf upon its side; but since that period, a grant was made by Parliament, and a voluntary subscription entered into for the formation of the present useful and safe road, "the most sublime terrace in the British Isles." It is guarded on the sea-side by a wall of about five feet high, add supported in many parts by deep walls below.—See pages 5 and 15.

PUFFIN ISLAND, OR PRIESTHOLME.

This uninhabited island is of an oval shape, about a mile in length, and half a mile in breadth. Near the centre is an old square tower, supposed to be the fragment of a religious house. During the summer the island swarms with various birds of passage, particularly the *alca artica*, or puffin. The firing of a gun will frequently cause clouds of these birds to rise, uttering loud and dissonant sounds.

PENRHYN CASTLE.

This edifice is supposed to stand upon the site of a palace, which, in the eighth century, belonged to Roderic Mwynog, grandson to Cadwalader, the last king of the Ancient Britons. It appears to have been rebuilt in the reign of Henry VI.; and although it has been greatly altered of late, the original design has been preserved. It is fronted with yellow brick, which gives it the appearance of stone. The gateway into the park resembles a Roman triumphal arch.

BEAUMARIS.

This pleasant little town is the capital of the island of Anglesea. Its name is formed from the French words *beau*, fair, and *marais*, marsh. The Castle was built by Edward I. towards the close of the thirteenth century, and its ruins are now included in the domains of Lady Bulkeley. On the accession of Charles II. Lord Bulkeley was Constable of the Castle. The lowness of its site, and the great diameter of its circular towers and bastions, together with the dilapidated state of its walls, deprive this structure, though exceedingly ponderous, of that prominent character and imposing effect so strikingly apparent in the prouder piles of Carnarvon and Conway. The town sends one member to Parliament.

BANGOR.

This is a Bishop's see, in the county of Carnarvon, and is said to derive its name from *bon*, good, and *chœur*, choir; but this seems a strained etymology. It is supposed to have been formerly a more considerable place than it is at present. The views from the elevated environs are extremely fine. The Cathedral was founded in the sixth century, by St. Deiniol (Daniel) who was elected the first Bishop of Bangor. It was destroyed by the Saxons in 1071, and rebuilt by King John in 1212. In 1402 it was burnt down, in the rebellion of Owen Glyndwr, and remained in ruins upwards of ninety years. It was rebuilt early in the sixteenth century, chiefly by Bishop Sheffington. On a rocky eminence, about half a mile east from Bangor, formerly stood a castle, built by Hugh, Earl of Chester, in the reign of William II. Its site is still visible. The situation of the Bishop's residence is much admired.

THE CHAIN-BRIDGE.

For a description of this magnificent and truly surprising structure, see pages 12 to 14.

CARNARVON.

This place is so called from *Caer*, a fortress, *yn*, in, and *Arfon*, the district opposite to Mon, or Anglesea. The ancient city was the only station possessed by the Romans in this part of Wales; it stood about half a mile south of the present town, where, probably, the British dwelt. The Castle is a magnificent ruin. It was built by Edward I. after the completion of his conquest in 1282; and as the Welsh would not submit quietly to be governed by any but a Welsh Prince, he caused his Queen (Eleanor) to reside here for a time, and here Edward II. was born. The Castle has been the scene of many memorable events, and is well worth an hour's contemplation. Carnarvon sends one member to Parliament.—See page 8.

DOL BADERN CASTLE.

This small but conspicuous structure is the only one remaining of five military stations erected by the Ancient Britons to defend the five passes through the Carnarvonshire chain of mountains.—See page 10.

SNOWDON.

The Snowdon range of mountains commences at Penmaen-mawr, and terminates on the margin of Carnarvon bay. The height of the peak of Snowdon is 3568 feet.

CONWAY.

Conway (from *Cynwy*, great river) is a fine old fortified town, situated at the northern corner of Carnarvonshire. The Castle was built in 1284, by Edward I. as a security against insurrections. He was besieged in it, and only rescued by the arrival of his fleet. In the civil wars in the seventeenth century it was garrisoned by the Archbishop of York, and afterwards by Prince Rupert. The town and Castle were taken by storm in 1646, but the parliamentary forces did not injure the Castle, which was never greatly damaged, until the Earl of Conway, who received a grant of it from Charles II. despoiled it of timber, lead, iron, &c. for his own use. A stranger will be much struck by the general appearance of Conway, which forms an interesting picture, and is very unlike any other place in the kingdom.—See page 16.

The writer of "the Trip" had no opportunity of visiting Capel Cerig, or Beddgelert; but no person should omit to do so when time will permit. From Carnarvon a most delightful tour may be made to Beddgelert, Capel Cerig, Snowdon, Llanberris lake, and back to Carnarvon.

CAPEL CERIG.

This village is said to have been called Capel Curig, in consequence of St. Curig being the patron of the chapel. From this place Snowdon and all the contiguous mountains burst at once full in view, marking this the finest approach to our boasted Alps. The scenery in the neighbourhood is full of variety and beauty.

BEDDGELERT.

This romantic village is said to derive its name from a singular occurrence. Tradition says, that Llewellyn the Great came to reside at Beddgelert during the hunting season, with his wife and children, and one day, the family being absent, a wolf had entered the house. On returning, his greyhound, called Cilihart, met him, wagging his tail, but covered with blood. The prince being alarmed, ran into the nursery, and found the cradle in which the child had lain overturned, and the ground covered with gore. Imagining the greyhound had killed the child, he immediately drew his sword and slew him; but, on turning up the cradle, he found under it the child alive, and the wolf dead. This so affected the prince, that he erected a tomb over his faithful dog's grave, where, afterwards, the parish-church was built, and called from this accident, Bedd-Cilihart, or The Grave of Cilihart. This incident gave rise to the following pathetic verses:

THE GRAVE OF THE GREYHOUND.

The spearmen heard the bugle sound,
   And cheer'ly smiled the morn,
And many a breach, and many a hound
   Attend Llewellyn's horn.

And still he blew a louder blast,
   And gave a louder cheer,
"Come, Gelert, why art thou the last
   Llewellyn's horn to hear?

"O where does faithful Gelert roam!
   The flow'r of all his race:
So true, so brave,—a lamb at home,
   A lion in the chase!"

'Twas only at Llewellyn's board
   The faithful Gelert fed;
He watch'd, he serv'd, he cheer'd his lord,
   And sentinel'd his bed.

In sooth he was a peerless hound,
   The gift of Royal John:
But now no Gelert could be found,
   And all the chase rode on.

And now as over rocks and dells
   The gallant chidings rise.
All Snowdon's craggy chaos yells,
   With many mingled cries.

That day Llewellyn little lov'd
   The chase of hart or hare,
And scant and small the booty proved,
   For Gelert was not there.

Unpleas'd Llewellyn homeward hied,
   When, near the portal seat,
His truant Gelert he espied,
   Bounding, his lord to greet.

But when he gain'd the Castle door,
   Aghast the chieftain stood—
The hound was smear'd with gouts of gore
   His lips and fangs ran blood!

Llewellyn gazed with wild surprise;
  Unus'd such looks to meet;
His fav'rite check'd his joyful guise,
  And crouch'd and lick'd his feet.

Onward in haste Llewellyn past,
  And on went Gelert too;
And still where'er his eyes he cast,
  Fresh blood gouts shock'd his view.

O'erturned his infant's bed he found,
  The blood-stain'd covert rent;
And all around the walls and ground,
  With recent blood besprent.

He call'd his child—no voice replied—
  He search'd with terror wild;
Blood, blood, he found on every side,
  But nowhere found the child;

"Hell-hound, by thee my child's devour'd,"
  The frantic father cried,
And to the hilt his vengeful sword
  He plunged in Gelert's side.

His suppliant, as to earth he fell,
  No pity could impart;
But still his Gelert's dying yell,
  Past heavy o'er his heart.

Arous'd by Gelert's dying yell,
  Some slumb'rer waken'd nigh;
What words the parent's joy can tell,
  To hear his infant cry!

Conceal'd beneath a mangled heap;
  His hurried search had miss'd,
All glowing from his rosy sleep,
  His cherub boy he kiss'd.

No scratch had he, nor harm nor dread;
  But, the same couch beneath,
Lay a great wolf, all torn and dead,
  Tremendous still in death!

Ah, what was then Llewellyn's pain,
  For now the truth was clear;

The gallant hound the wolf had slain,
  To save Llewellyn's heir.

Vain, vain, was all Llewellyn's woe:
  "Best of thy kind adieu:
The frantic deed that laid thee low,
  This heart shall ever rue."

And now a gallant tomb they raise,
  With costly sculpture deck'd;
And marbles storied with his praise,
  Poor Gelert's bones protect.

Here never could the spearmen pass,
  Or forester unmov'd;
Here oft the tear-besprinkled grass,
  Llewellyn's sorrow prov'd.

And here he hung his horn and spear—
  And oft as evening fell,
In fancy's piercing sounds would hear
  Poor Gelert's dying yell!

And till great Snowdon's rocks grow old,
  And cease the storm to brave,
The consecrated spot shall hold
  The name of Gelert's grave!

FINIS.

Milton Keynes UK
Ingram Content Group UK Ltd.
UKHW031630231024
450082UK00005B/466